A DICTIONARY
of ANIMAL SYMBOLS

M.V. MONTGOMERY

Winter Goose
Publishing

Winter Goose Publishing
2701 Del Paso Road, 130-92
Sacramento, CA 95835

www.wintergoosepublishing.com
Contact Information: info@wintergoosepublishing.com

A Dictionary of Animal Symbols

COPYRIGHT © 2014 by MV Montgomery

ISBN: 978-1-941058-12-1

First Edition, April 2014

Cover Art by Winter Goose Publishing
Typeset by Odyssey Books

Published in the United States of America

Acknowledgments: Some of these poems first appeared online in *Willow Springs* and *Barometric Pressures* (Kind of a Hurricane Press Author's Series).

To my mom,
Donna Lagorio Montgomery

and to Tim,
who is always covering for me

Contents

Albatross, Spirit, Stamina   1
Ant, Industry, Diligence   2
Ape, Vanity, Imitation   3
Bat, Night, Fear   4
Bear, Ancestry, Prophecy   5
Bee, Devoutness, Duty   6
Boar, Ferocity, Courage   7
Buffalo, Whirlwind, Plenitude   8
Bull, Potency, Life Force   9
Butterfly, Soul, Psyche   10
Camel, Stoicism, Sobriety   11
Chameleon, Thunder, Rain   12
Cicada, Aging, Debility   13
Cow, Maternity, Nurturing   14
Coyote, Scavenging, Mischief   15
Crab, Wavering, Backtracking   16
Crane, Contemplation, Beauty   17
Crocodile, Ill-Temper, Destruction   18
Crow, Hope, Despair   19
Cuckoo, Opportunity, Riches   20
Dolphin, Sea-Change, Playfulness   21
Donkey, Humility, Obstinacy   22
Dove, Peace, Love   23
Duck, Happiness, Fidelity   24
Dugong, Transformation, Feminine Allure   25
Eagle, Majesty, Dominion   26
Elephant, Chastity, Longevity   27
Flea, Pestilence, Aversion   28
Frog, Metamorphosis, Ontogeny   29
Giraffe, Shyness, Reserve   30
Goat, Lust, Devil   31
Goose, Loquaciousness, Friendliness   32
Hare, Reproduction, the Trinity   33

Hedgehog, Ingenuity, Gluttony   34
Horse, River, Sun   35
Jackal, Embalming, Decay   36
Lion, Divine Radiance, Fury   37
Lynx, Acuity, Vision   38
Monkey, Childishness, Curiosity   39
Octopus, Stealth, Hypnosis   40
Ostrich, Justice, Avoidance   41
Owl, Wisdom, Death   42
Ox, Strength, Patience   43
Parrot, Repetition, Oracularity   44
Peacock, Immortality, Pride   45
Pelican, Self-Sacrifice, Christ   46
Pig, Greediness, Libido   47
Rat, Self-Preservation, Resourcefulness   48
Rhinoceros, Protection, Scholarship   49
Robin, Empathy, the Passion   50
Rooster, Vigilance, Virility   51
Scorpion, Retribution, Give-and-Take   52
Snake, Energy, Deceit   53
Spider, Destiny, Entrapment   54
Stag, Tree, Vitality   55
Stoat, Delicacy, Purity   56
Tiger, Wrath, Swiftness   57
Toad, Witchcraft, Toxicity   58
Tortoise, Patience, Stability   59
Vulture, Gatekeeping, Life Cycle   60
Whale, Rite of Passage, Rebirth   61
Wolf, Wildness, Surrogacy   62

Index   63
About the Author   65

Albatross, Spirit, Stamina

Angel of death,
white-winged,
the albatross is
readily available
to make stops
out at sea
for lost sailors—

No matter how far
those souls
may have drifted.

Ant, Industry, Diligence

Once fed to
listless patients
in Morocco
as a specific for

slow metabolism,
a dose of ant
is said to rouse
the spirits to dance.

And if that
singular approach
doesn't work,
try the pants.

Ape, Vanity, Imitation

Ape was always other,
our tag-along brother.

Painters tried to blame
him for original sin
by placing an apple
in his mouth—

Fortunately for us,
the ape could not
thus protest his own
innocence.

Bat, Night, Fear

Nailed to doors
to ward off demons,
bats were deployed
to fight fear with fear.

Devourers of light,
they ushered in
the gathering dusk
in swooping gulps.

Although once reputed
to possess strong vision,
this creature, inside,
is full of night.

Bear, Ancestry, Prophecy

Sleeping under a bearskin
at night will summon
dark dreams.

Wearing a bear mask
emboldens one to address
forest familiars.

Bear is the guise shamans
put on to see what
lies ahead.

Bee, Devoutness, Duty

Essene priests were said
to buzz about the hive
of the Church.

Sweet is the path of belief,
but so often marked
with nettles.

Boar, Ferocity, Courage

When the battle grows thick,
send in the helmeted boars!

They will scrum with gusto
and root out the very demons
from the soil. Yes—

When the sides are picked,
I bet on the boars.

Buffalo, Whirlwind, Plenitude

It might take plenty
to stir a top-heavy bison
from its bed
in prairie grass—

But when the herd
begins to move,
a thundering
whirlwind rises,

and a dust cloud
may be traced
across the flatland
for miles.

Bull, Potency, Life Force

To seize the bull's horns
is to seize the day,
to rush bellowing
into that good night,

not to dodge one's desires
with the usual feints
and ruses.

For the victor—
a shower in bull's blood.

Butterfly, Soul, Psyche

When
a butterfly
is reborn
from its
chrysalis-
cave,
it appears
to leave
solid mass
behind,
becoming
airy
on
the wing,
drifting
silent
as
thought.

Camel, Stoicism, Sobriety

The camel picks itself up
and dusts itself off,

ceases its complaining
and shoulders its burden,

always understanding that
its life-journey is not easy,

and no drinks will be served.

Chameleon, Thunder, Rain

A storm can
come on quickly,
light-to-dark,
a sudden burst—

So too the
changeable chameleon,
who with wild
eyes spiraling

climbs higher up
a branch for safety,
testing the air
with lightning tongue.

Cicada, Aging, Debility

The desiccated husk
of the cicada
serves as our reminder
not to wish to live
too long.

Tithonus married
immortal Eos,
but that sip of ambrosia
only kept him alive
as he withered on.

Now his constant calls
to his wife have become
a senile drone,
a mute plea for death,
a wish to be gone.

Cow, Maternity, Nurturing

This earth mother
is quite psychedelic—
her crescent horns
may suggest the moon,
her milk the galaxy.

Our surrogate,
nursing us long after
we have weaned—
and tutor, helping to
familiarize the skies.

Coyote, Scavenging, Mischief

A coyote can rearrange
a campsite quickly
by dragging off supplies
in its teeth.

If chastised, it will
retreat, tongue lolling
in a panting grin.

Pursuit is pointless.

Crab, Wavering, Backtracking

Was it courage
for the crab
to pinch at the heels
of Hercules?

Considering the hero
was otherwise
preoccupied
with the Hydra?

The reader
may be excused
for going back and forth
on such questions.

Crane, Contemplation, Beauty

Just what
sort of
yogi
is the crane,
contorting
deftly
in its
mating
dance,
posing
steadily
on one leg
in meditative
posture,
pronouncing
its speech-
sembling
mantras?

Much
we could
learn
from such
a teacher,
if ever
we could
sit at
one's feet.

Crocodile, Ill-Temper, Destruction

A crocodile sets traps
in its teeth and appears,
to all the world,
to be asleep.

Egyptian gods were fond
of borrowing its jaws
to eat out the hearts
of enemies.

Crow, Hope, Despair

Nothing divides so
much as a crow—
some see ill-omen,
others a boon.

Prophets divide us
in similar ways—
we only welcome
pleasant visions.

When predictions
go wrong, however,
it may become time
to eat crow.

Cuckoo, Opportunity, Riches

When you see a cuckoo,
better guard your nest egg.

But if you heed its advice,
you might never beg.

Either follow the cuckoo
if it knows more than you do,

or escape poco-a-poco,
because that bird is loco.

Dolphin, Sea-Change, Playfulness

What do you do
with a drunken sailor?
Perhaps turn him
into a dolphin.

So Bacchus did,
before casting
his new play-mate
upon the jaunty waves.

Donkey, Humility, Obstinacy

Jesus indeed chose a lean
machine, though he might have
needed a tow.

When stuck in the mud, this
no-frills ride might just decide
not to go.

Dove, Peace, Love

Doves are born in the throats
of martyrs, become moans in
the mouths of lovers, and are
then swallowed by politicians,
who close their lips to all hope.

Duck, Happiness, Fidelity

At this marriage
of sky and water,
I pronounce you
duck and duck.

You may now
swim off
together,
in perfect synch.

Dugong, Transformation, Feminine Allure

Sea-brides for sailors
who've been out too long—
Yo, ho, bring a man down.

Seeming to sing a
seductive love song—
Yo, ho, bring a man down.

Graceful and shapely
upon distant shores—
Yo ho, bring a man down.

Many's the fool who has
plunged overboard—
Yo, ho, bring a man down.

Eagle, Majesty, Dominion

The Romans released
an eagle
from the pyres
of emperors,

for only such
a brazen bird
could fly straight
into the sun,

unblinking,
ferrying souls
to the highest
heaven.

Elephant, Chastity, Longevity

The bull elephant was said
to remain chaste for his mate
and to stay at her side for life.

True, to hide an indiscretion
would be quite a feat.

Flea, Pestilence, Aversion

I think that
I shall never see
a creature lonely
as the flea.

Frog, Metamorphosis, Ontogeny

Frogs recapitulate
the way we began—
from embryo to tadpole,
from water to land.

Giraffe, Shyness, Reserve

Zarafa, said to be a charmer
once was led through Paris,
a gift from Egypt to the king,
attracting a large crowd of
100,000 underlings—

Who climbed trees to get a
better look at the lanky star
that soon would inspire
fads in clothing and hair.

Zarafa had no comment on
this occasion, confirming
long-held views that he and
his brethren were mute.

But we know better today—
like many future celebrities,
Zarafa simply had nothing
much important to say.

Goat, Lust, Devil

I have tested the
devil-bearded one,
heard stories

of kicking hooves
bringing about
great destruction,

of vile lust, and
of orneriness raised
to metaphysical rage,

yet always found him
kin to lamb. So let us
praise the goat.

Goose, Loquaciousness, Friendliness

One might have mixed feelings
having such a gossip for a friend—
one who can't keep silent
and sometimes gets a bit silly.

Yet there is no denying the bird
can be quite pleasant company—
particularly if invited to be part
of the Christmas feast.

Hare, Reproduction, the Trinity

Three hares in a circle
found in a prayer room.
Three hares sharing three ears,
yet each one has two.

Three hares in a circle
high on a church roof.
Three hares sharing three ears,
Yet each one has two.

Three hares in a circle
slow turning the moon.
Three hares sharing three ears,
yet each one has two.

Hedgehog, Ingenuity, Gluttony

The hedgehog rolls
into a ball, knocking its food
from the vine.

It then skewers the fruit
like a true gourmand,
on its bristly behind.

Horse, River, Sun

The flow of a horse
is its mane.

A running horse
is relentless,
hooves barely
touching the soil.

A wild horse
rearing in silhouette
is suddenly
outlined in light.

Jackal, Embalming, Decay

Jackal-headed Anubis
was the god of embalming—

Ironic, given this predator's
notorious reputation for
ever-reeking of death.

Lion, Divine Radiance, Fury

Although a nocturnal hunter
and a lover of shade, the gold-
maned lion was considered
both resurrection and light.

Cubs, born blind, were thought
to be dead for three days until
awakened by their fathers—
hence the Easter association.

Yet scores of Christian martyrs
would surely have preferred
to have kept the ferocious cat
at a much safer distance.

Lynx, Acuity, Vision

The lynx is acute
on a stakeout,
pacing patiently,
its coat of spots
apt camouflage,
its eyes two
penetrating beams.

It can tail a suspect
over snow and ice,
paws padded
for stealth, until
muscles tense,
and kit moves in
for the kill.

Monkey, Childishness, Curiosity

Monkey see,
monkey do.

Monkcy hcar,
monkey try.

Monkey speak,
monkey want—

Discretion is
the better part
of monkey!

Octopus, Stealth, Hypnosis

Don't be a sucker
for the octopus,
which veils its escapes
        in ink—

        And swims
with a pulsing motion,
both progress
        and a retreat—

And twirls
its long arms
like a vortex,
        hyp-nautical-ly.

Ostrich, Justice, Avoidance

Ma'at, the goddess of justice,
used an ostrich's even feathers
to weigh out the hearts of the dead,
testing the heaviness of their sins.

If ever present at such weigh-ins,
no doubt this noncommittal bird
must have turned its head away.

Owl, Wisdom, Death

Who
would wish to see
what an owl sees at night?

What
graveyard goings-on,
what plots of men and mice?

Where
forest kills are common,
and whatever is, is right?

Ox, Strength, Patience

Paradoxically, the ox
with its great fortitude,
is found to be quite docile.

Paradoxically, the ox,
a symbol of enlightenment,
becomes our simile for dumb.

Parrot, Repetition, Oracularity

The parrot offers
indisputable proof—
how portentous
our own words
start to sound when
repeated back to us.

Peacock, Immortality, Pride

Vision of the divine,
hundred-eyed beauty
praised as immortal,
the peacock has sipped
from a golden chalice
it chooses not to share.

Pelican, Self-Sacrifice, Christ

The mother pelican
was thought to tear
her breast to restore
dead chicks with her
blood, *that they may
have life.* Depicted
in her nest, she was
said to be *in her piety.*

Ironic that this holy
bird, which inspired
patriarchs such as
Aquinas and Dante
to refer to Jesus as
the *Good Pelican*, or
Our Pelican, was both
female and a mother.

Pig, Greediness, Libido

To eat too much pig
is to be in danger of
becoming one.

Know when to stop,
when to be happy
in your poke.

Rat, Self-Preservation, Resourcefulness

Follow the rat
That always senses when a ship
will go down in a storm.

Follow the rat
That finds the way to rich stores
when provisions are spare.

Follow the rat
That forever wins the life-race,
passing on many descendants.

Rhinoceros, Protection, Scholarship

Stories once told of the powerful magic
      in a rhino's powdered horn. It was said
            to detect poison, and to protect the user
                  from harm. Reports spread to several
                        countries of this marvelous talisman,
                            and may have served as
                              the foundation of
                                our myths of
                                unicorns.

Robin, Empathy, the Passion

A robin's tap at the window
was said to herald death.

At the Passion, the bird felt pity,
plucking thorns from the Savior's head.

And this was the reason given
for its breast being splashed with red.

Rooster, Vigilance, Virility

The rooster struts,
cocksure that
its crowing
calls off darkness.

Watchful
in all directions,
preserving his
frightened harem—

If only he
wasn't so over-wound
at such an
impossible hour!

Scorpion, Retribution, Give-and-Take

The scorpion
carries a deadly venom,
but was thought to secrete
a healing antidote.

So, if you were
prepared to meet its terms,
your life might not be
immediately forfeit.

Snake, Energy, Deceit

A coiled snake
generates its own
electricity.

It can swallow
the whole earth,
or feast on its
own tail—

Or stretch out
like lightning,
then dissemble
and be gone.

Spider, Destiny, Entrapment

The world of illusion, *Maya*,
is the spider's delicate web.

We lose ourselves in desire,
always too caught up to care.

Fortune may drop from heaven,
on a single gossamer thread—

It remains for us to ascend,
and not get caught in a snare.

Stag, Tree, Vitality

The stag grows
new branches
each spring,

and magically
finds its way
to healing herbs.

It is said to be
a favorite of fairies.

Stoat, Delicacy, Purity

The fragile stoat
was thought to die
if its winter coat
got muddy,

and judges once
wore ermine trim
so justice wouldn't
turn bloody.

Tiger, Wrath, Swiftness

He who dares
ride a tiger
had better be a god.

Otherwise,
the tiger decides
who lives or dies.

Toad, Witchcraft, Toxicity

The bulge of a toad's
throat is the moon,
and inside its head
a night-jewel.

A toad lives
in Middle-earth
and only comes out
in foul weather.

Its lip is curled from
the poison it brews.

Tortoise, Patience, Stability

How fortunate for us
the tortoise,

which anchors the world
and all its rancor

upon its mighty back,
cannot slack

its yeoman duties readily,
and remains steady.

Vulture, Gatekeeping, Life Cycle

Vultures are forever
present at both ends:
as protective mothers,
as hasteners of decay.

Necessarily, so the cycle
can play itself out again.

Whale, Rite of Passage, Rebirth

A whale makes a most
pleasant accommodation,

where one may wait out
dark phases of the moon.

One may tap its fine teeth
with a hammer, or spelunk

about its ample belly—
looking forward, of course,

to ultimate deliverance.

Wolf, Wildness, Surrogacy

Though big & bad
in nursery rhyme
the wolf is sociable,
among its own kind—

And raises lost wood-
whelps until they get on,
from Romulus & Remus
to Genghis Khan.

Index

Acuity	see Lynx	Imitation	see Ape
Aging	see Cicada	Immortality	see Peacock
Ancestry	see Bear	Industry	see Ant
Aversion	see Flea	Ingenuity	see Hedgehog
Avoidance	see Ostrich	Justice	see Ostrich
Backtracking	see Crab	Libido	see Pig
Beauty	see Crane	Life Cycle	see Vulture
Chastity	see Elephant	Life Force	see Bull
Childishness	see Monkey	Longevity	see Elephant
Christ	see Pelican	Loquaciousness	see Goose
Contemplation	see Crane	Love	see Dove
Courage	see Boar	Lust	see Goat
Curiosity	see Monkey	Majesty	see Eagle
Death	see Owl	Maternity	see Cow
Debility	see Cicada	Metamorphosis	see Frog
Decay	see Jackal	Mischief	see Coyote
Deceit	see Snake	Night	see Bat
Delicacy	see Stoat	Nurturing	see Cow
Despair	see Crow	Obstinacy	see Donkey
Destiny	see Spider	Ontogeny	see Frog
Destruction	see Crocodile	Opportunity	see Cuckoo
Devil	see Goat	Oracularity	see Parrot
Devoutness	see Bee	the Passion	see Robin
Diligence	see Ant	Patience	see Tortoise
Divine Radiance	see Lion	Peace	see Dove
Dominion	see Eagle	Pestilence	see Flea
Duty	see Bee	Playfulness	see Dolphin
Embalming	see Jackal	Plenitude	see Buffalo
Empathy	see Robin	Potency	see Bull
Energy	see Snake	Pride	see Peacock
Entrapment	see Spider	Prophecy	see Bear
Fear	see Bat	Protection	see Rhinoceros
Feminine Allure	see Dugong	Psyche	see Butterfly
Ferocity	see Boar	Purity	see Stoat
Fidelity	see Duck	Rain	see Chameleon
Friendliness	see Goose	Rebirth	see Whale
Fury	see Lion	Repetition	see Parrot
Gatekeeping	see Vulture	Reproduction	see Hare
Gluttony	see Hedgehog	Reserve	see Giraffe
Give-and-Take	see Scorpion	Resourcefulness	see Rat
Greediness	see Pig	Retribution	see Scorpion
Happiness	see Duck	Riches	see Cuckoo
Hope	see Crow	River	see Horse
Humility	see Donkey	Rite of Passage	see Whale
Hypnosis	see Octopus	Scavenging	see Coyote
Ill-Temper	see Crocodile	Scholarship	see Rhinoceros

Sea-Change	see Dolphin
Self-preservation	see Rat
Self-Sacrifice	see Pelican
Shyness	see Giraffe
Sobriety	see Camel
Soul	see Butterfly
Swiftness	see Tiger
Spirit	see Albatross
Stability	see Tortoise
Stamina	see Albatross
Stealth	see Octopus
Stoicism	see Camel
Sun	see Horse
Surrogacy	see Wolf
Thunder	see Chameleon
Toxicity	see Toad
Transformation	see Dugong
Tree	see Stag
the Trinity	see Hare
Vanity	see Ape
Vigilance	see Rooster
Virility	see Rooster
Vision	see Lynx
Vitality	see Stag
Wavering	see Crab
Whirlwind	see Buffalo
Wildness	see Wolf
Wisdom	see Owl
Witchcraft	see Toad
Wrath	see Tiger

About the Author

M.V. Montgomery is a professor at Life University in Atlanta and the author of three previous books of poetry: *Joshu Holds a Press Conference, Strange Conveyances*, and *What We Did With Old Moons*.

His author site is mvmontgomery.wordpress.com.

POETRY *by M. V. Montgomery*

JOSHU HOLDS A PRESS CONFERENCE

"M V Montgomery's thoughtful poems are glimpses of historical moments, by turns moving, perceptive, haunting and funny. A pleasure to read, and an education."

—Alex von Tunzelmann, *The Guardian*

"One thing that's impossible to argue with in M V Montgomery's *Joshu Holds A Press Conference* is its ambition—in essence he presents us with a history of the world from Hercules to Barack Obama told by way of biographies in verse . . . an admirable project."

—Declan Ryan, *Poetry London*

"It is good to have a guide who is full of bonhomie, not immune to the occasional bout of horror and misery, but always consumed by the thrill of our wide, wonderful world, with its heroes, murderers, poets, prophets, wackos, monarchs, artists, adventurers and paragons, and the spectacular concatenation of legends that is their constantly spreading wake."

—Christopher Hobday, *The Conversation Papers*

STRANGE CONVEYANCES

"Like a character from a magical realist novel, Montgomery's speaker never thinks any situation to be bizarre. And like Camus's Mersault, he never has reservations about his present predicament. But though it is interesting to draw these parallels, it would be irresponsible to call *Strange Conveyances* either absurdist or magical realist. It is a book about dreams, and . . . no greater proof exists in the contemporary literary world of how captivating the dreams of another can be."

—Benjamin C. Krause, *Muscle & Blood Magazine*

"Montgomery's poetry is real and accessible—not the poetry of angst buried in dark corners, but the work of one who lives with eyes open."

—Amy L. George, *Bird's Eye reView*

"In *Strange Conveyances*, a real world is evoked. Within the re-enactment, the recollection, the facsimile, the poet goes about his mysterious business. In the manner of the last man cataloguing the universe for whatever might follow mankind, or an American Proust discovering himself in the lingering images of memory like a ghost on the edge of a photograph, Montgomery is both the wise, mundivagant sage and the baseball-capped friend at the bar, discussing the wonderful machinations of existence with the easy tones of a close friend shooting the breeze about the weekend ballgame. Like any gifted interlocutor's, his reports are personal, but universal; the inner logic of the poetry, with its philosophical clarity and ensuing verisimilitude, never fails to reveal emotional or psychological truths that are impossible to deny—thanks in the main to a charming and overarching benevolence."

—Christopher Hobday, *The Conversation Papers*

WHAT WE DID WITH OLD MOONS

"Whimsical, never heavy-handed, yet still showing a great depth of emotion, Montgomery's collection is a wonderful catalog of longing, brimming with histories—both real and imagined—that will enchant until the very end."

—Robert James Russell, *Midwestern Gothic*

"M.V. Montgomery's poems are funny, contemporary, and clever."

—Philip Vermaas, *Misfits' Miscellany*

"If F. Scott Fitzgerald hadn't sometimes bored me to tears, his name would have been M.V. Montgomery."

—Cole Knight, *Circus of the Damned*

www.ingramcontent.com/pod-product-compliance
Lightning Source LLC
Chambersburg PA
CBHW031632040426
42452CB00007B/797